COL
BLIND

My late wife Annette, and me

Ken Rigney

Contents

Dedication .... *v*

Introduction .... *vi*

My happy childhood *1*

    Meeting John MacBean *10*

The Riots in 1949 .... *22*

Starting work *24*

Becoming a father *27*

Tragedy (My brother's suicide) *28*

Break-up *32*

Deciding to leave *34*

Becoming British *39*

Joining the Merchant Navy *43*

Bringing Ashley to Britain *47*

Fulfilling a promise *51*

Buying a house *53*

Blind date *64*

True Saints Fan 66

Days of wine and roses 69

My journey with Agapanthus, Crocosmia and
Lavatera Flowering Plants 74

Crocosmia Golden Ballerina 81

Midnight Madness 89

The Apartheid Laws and how they affected families' lives 94

Dedication

Peter, if you hadn't agreed to leave South Africa and accompany me to the UK, I might not have done so on my own. We both embarked on a journey to the land of our forefathers, even though our families thought we were crazy. In the end it fulfilled both our dreams, so thank you, Peter, it changed both our futures for the better. Even though you're not here to read this, I'm sure Pam, Charlotte and Jemma are so proud of you and what you achieved.

Peter

Acknowledgements

My thank you to:

My Grandparents – *Albert* and *Eleanor Stoffels (Big Daddy and Tuku Mama)*

My Parents – *Willy* and *Amy Rigney*

Aunt Vi and *Aunt Peggy*

For my happy childhood

And in the UK:

Dr Tim Morgan of Regents Park Surgery and Shirley Health Centre for listening, advising and helping to keep me in good health.

Fred and *Hazel Blake*, my friends since arriving in the UK

Owen and *Ann Drumgoole*, my good friends and neighbours especially at the time of the Midnight Madness incident.

Last but not least – *Patrick Fairweather*, his two Girl Fridays – *Sharon Lowndes* and *Lisa Smith* – at the Nursery where I spent and where I still spend many happy hours.

Introduction

Because I only recently decided to write my life story and never having had a diary or written notes, everything in this book is from memory and written as accurately as I can recall. At first it was just going to be something short for my great-grandchildren to read, but as I started writing I began reliving my life and this is the result. I hope it will be enjoyed by all who read it.

Colour-Blind

My happy childhood

I was born on March 12th 1930 in Durban, South Africa. My mother and the midwife first thought I was stillborn as I didn't show any signs of life. I was put in cold water and then warm, and eventually I gave a feeble cry. Because of this I was very sickly as a child and my mum told me there were times when she didn't think I'd survive. We had a wood and coal stove in those days and I can remember as I grew older, she would put newspaper in the oven, then put my vest on it to warm it. School was approximately three miles away. After it had been raining there'd be puddles and we'd take off our shoes to walk through them. If my mum knew she'd have hit the roof, but gradually I overcame my chest and other

Me with Pointer hunting dog

medical problems.

I started school at the age of six. It was a mixed race school of all denominations: Catholic, Protestant, Jewish and Muslim. The school building was in the shape of the letter 'L'. On the right hand side was another long building. The top half was used for the girls' cookery and sewing classes, and the other half for the boys' DIY and woodworking classes. It was also used for concerts and film (bioscope) shows.

Our headmaster, Mr Nero, music teacher Miss Hallum and the two teachers who taught cookery and DIY were white, while the rest of the staff were (when I think about it now) fair skinned and of mixed race. During my school years I was oblivious of the different colours of the community in which I lived and the differences of the pupils and the staff at my school. It was only when I left school to start working and how it affected me that I started to realise the difference. Hence my description of the staff at my first school.

We were given fresh milk daily, and my friends and I used our coronation mugs, which we were given when King George was crowned in 1937. Of course our mugs were bigger than the ones that were handed out, and since they belonged to us we looked after them. I remember we'd add brown sugar to the milk. I'll have to try it again one day, but I'm sure I won't like it.

We had a parents' day once a year. I really looked forward to that. I was in the boys' 'Drill Brigade'. There were about 30 of us. We'd start from behind the school, then march into the quadrangle, and come in at an angle. The first boy, then the second, and so on. The highlight was to be in the front row and being the first. I never did make the first but did make second.

We were marching to music, with all the parents and the rest of the school watching. I remember seeing my mum and the proud look on her face, even more so when I sang solo. It was the song from Shakespeare's 'The Tempest' (Where the bee sucks, there suck I), and I still know all the words.

The parents visited all the classrooms, seeing what their children had done: drawings, cakes, wooden trays etc. They were encouraged to buy them for a nominal price. This was how the school was able to buy the instruments for the percussion band, and a projector and screen to show films in the assembly hall. I think our school was one of the most progressive in the city even though it was situated in one of the poorest suburbs in Durban.

I took singing lessons from the new teacher who was called Mrs Blackaby, and the highlight of this was me singing in the Natal Eisteddfod, which was held in Durban City Hall. Unfortunately, not long after this my voice started breaking and I couldn't reach the high notes. I then lost interest and never sang in public again, much to Mum's disappointment. After sitting my primary school certificate exam at the age of thirteen, I left and went on to high school.

One of the highlights of my growing up period was in the mid 1930s when the motorcycle Grand Prix was run. The starting line was right where my grandfather had his tearoom (eating house). Before the race started we'd go to the top of the hill and then the riders would come up to where we were and then descend, travel along the flat road (where the oil refinery is now located) and then up the Marine Drive. Then to Brighton Beach, the Bluff, and back again. In all, about twelve miles.

I still remember the names of some of the riders and their bikes. There was Don Hall, Dave Ware, John Galway and Chuck Harris – I always thought he was a bit fat to be a rider, but I could have been wrong. I was only eight years old.

Some of the bikes were AJs, Velocette, Norton, but my favourite was the Triumph. There were also motorcycle sidecar races and hill climbs, which I enjoyed watching.

The first house I remember growing up in was situated in the middle of nowhere. My grandad, 'Big Daddy', built roads and also sold land for a large property firm in Durban. The plot of land was a third of an acre and my dad built a small wood and corrugated iron house. There was no running water or electricity. The toilet was quite a way from the house, being basic as you can imagine.

On the side of the house there was a massive tank that collected water from the gutter and I remember my dad pouring something on the top of the tank which he said prevented the mosquitoes from breeding. Mum insisted on the water being boiled before using it. (We had a galvanised bath in a shed, and this is how it was until my dad built the big house which had a proper bathroom and toilet.) Over the years five plots were sold, my grandad buying one himself and building what we called the really big house. Two other plots were bought for my two aunts.

My Grandad Albert Stoffels, "Big Daddy". A great influence on my life

As the area became more populated more homes and roads were built. My grandad, father, two uncles and a group of friends were keen huntsmen and every year (June, July, August, the hunting season), they would be invited to some of the big sugar plantations to hunt deer.

In the plantations were large orchards of oranges and bananas. Me, my brother Glen and a couple of other youngsters would accompany them because our job was to look after the hunting dogs. We'd be left in the orchard until the hunt was over. My dad

bred Harrier Beagles which were the best for sniffing out the deer.
(I also helped with the breeding programme.)

My Uncle Cecil, Big Daddy, Mum and Dad. Hunting
dogs, rifles and youngsters getting in on the act.

Whoever shot a deer had first choice of the skin and horns to
mount on a shield. My dad being one of the best of the rest, we had
skins on the floor and horns mounted on shields. My Uncle Fred
managed a tanning factory so the skins were all done professionally.
We were always eating venison (buck meat). Strangely enough it
doesn't taste the same now. Maybe it's because the deer here are
more or less domesticated.

During this period of my early teenage years, and even before, I
asked my mum when did she first start keeping chickens, because
from a very young age I can remember us having them. She said

she'd been given one as a present and one day she woke up to see it with a clutch of chicks. As there were no fowls (chickens) in the vicinity, it meant its previous owner kept roosters and hens together.

There were quite a few occasions when a hen appeared with her new chicks, but with one or two eggs left behind that hadn't yet hatched. I would notice a crack on the egg meaning the chick was trying to emerge. I'd carefully remove the shell, take the chick out, and gently rub it all over with a soft cloth until the feathers were all dry and fluffy. Because it would be unfamiliar to the mother (she'd peck it to death), I'd wait until nightfall, then put the chick under her with the others. Next morning it would be running around with its brothers and sisters with the mother none the wiser. I also used this method with my Moscovy ducks as well.

In hindsight maybe I really should have become a poultry farmer.

I became interested in breeding chickens. All my pocket money would go on buying eggs from purebred chickens to be hatched by my own hens. Actually, in South Africa everyone called chickens "fowls". Chickens were little chicks, hens were female adults and roosters, collectively fowls. Anyway, I bred Light Sussex, Rhode Island Reds, and Black Australorps. I also had Tumbler pigeons and rabbits which were called Belgian hares.

A small deer, which had somehow found its way into our back garden, became trapped. My father wanted to shoot it, but I insisted we try to catch it, which we did. It was a very small type of deer, which was probably a young Duiker. I called it Sally, not knowing whether it was male or female. It became quite tame, eating out of my hand. My dad was not happy about me keeping it though, because he said it would affect the dogs' sense of smell when they went hunting.

One day I came home from school and Sally wasn't there. My dad had given her away to friends; she died after two weeks. I think I hated my dad then for what he'd done.

The youngest of the Gunter Family were Christian, Hendrick and Sucky. Hendrick was my age but was much bigger than me in build. He had a dog called Wagter (pronounced Vu'g'ter) with a soft G. Roughly it meant 'Don't mess with me, I'm vicious'.

My dad came home one day with a black terrier dog. He never told us who gave it to him or why, and why he had agreed to have it, especially since the only dogs we had were hunting dogs. This dog was really vicious. We had a washing line between two poles and my dad tied him to this so he could run along it. No one could go near the dog and he was kept away from the other dogs. I called him Snapper and very slowly made friends with him.

My cousin Garner and I used to fetch milk from a friend of my grandad's who lived up the hill and who kept a couple of his cows. It was still dark early one morning when we decided to take Snapper with us, so we untied him and off we went. Everything was fine until we got back home. My dad was furious. My mum had to intervene and wanted to know if Snapper was always going to be tied up. From that day on Snapper was always by my side. But I had to make sure there weren't any strange dogs around as he wouldn't just sniff around them but would go straight on the attack. Strangely enough though, he tolerated our other dogs and they kept out of his way.

There were three occasions when Snapper tarnished his image of being a good dog. The first was when a man was walking along the road towards our house and he had a large red retriever alongside. I was sitting on the front verandah. The front door of our house was open and suddenly Snapper rushed out and made straight for the dog. I ran out to follow, to catch him, calling out to my mum. When I got there the man was trying to separate them and got bitten for his efforts. I managed to pull Snapper away. My mum then took the guy into the house to wash his wound and rub some antiseptic on it. Luckily it wasn't serious.

Not long after this, Mrs Gunter decided to come over to see my mum. Now, Mrs Gunter was a large woman even compared to my mum. Unknown to her, 'Wagter', Hendrick's dog, had started following her. She had just started climbing the steps when Snapper saw Wagter and attacked, without warning. I had to drag Snapper away. Mrs Gunter was nearly fainting and my mum was trying to steady her and help her up the last step, to sit her down. She kept saying to Mum, "Get me some smelling salts." [Is that right? I think I'll have to Google smelling salts!] Anyway, the result was no harm done. My mum said to me on both those occasions, "Don't mention this to your father." Of course I didn't: I didn't want to lose Snapper.

The third time I was sitting under the huge tree in front of the house with Snapper when suddenly Hendrick appeared with Wagter. Straight away the two dogs went for each other. Hendrick was quite confident and kept saying in Afrikaans "Vat hom, Wagter" – in other words, "Go get him". While I was saying in English "Go on, Snapper". Suddenly, as quick as it had started, Wagter slunk off. Hendrick gave me a dirty look and went off as well.

Snapper and I were as close as one boy and his dog can be, but one day he suddenly became ill and died soon afterwards. I remember running to my aunts and crying and telling them that Snapper had died. When my dad first brought him home he was already fully grown, so we had no idea how old he was. It could have been old age. I buried him at the bottom of the garden.

My dad never ever told us how he'd acquired the dog, who gave it to him and why. Especially when he was only interested in breeding hunting dogs. But I thank him for giving me Snapper.

Meeting John MacBean

Up on the hill, from where we used to watch the motorcycle races, a huge military base was built. (The last motorcycle race was run in 1939.) At this particular time there were many British sailors there. Some building blocks were given names such as HMS Assegai.

In front of our house was this large open field where we'd play football and other games. For the British guys going into town they'd have to walk across this field to get to the bus stop. One day while we were playing there, these two sailors started kicking the ball with us. (I suppose they had nothing to do in their spare time.) My mum called us and when she saw these two lads asked them if they would like to come in for a cup of tea. At the time, my cousin Ada was staying with us. She was around eighteen and quite attractive. After that these two guys were always making an excuse to pop in.

Eventually John MacBean came on his own as his friend had to leave, and then John himself left. But he did write to me asking how my chickens and rabbits were coming along. I remember his ship or submarine was HMS Maraga. I also remembered him telling me he was from Inverness and that he'd worked in the city's swimming baths. (Much of this later.) This was in 1941.

There are many events I can remember occurring during my childhood. Coming home from school one day I had to first pass my great-gran's home. She was Scottish and had married a Belgian. Everyone called her Mrs Stoffels, but I think in my conversations with her, she must have mentioned that she was a Strachan because I always called her Granny Strachan. (No one

Young Ken

else did. My Aunt Peggy who turned 100 on September 7th 2016 (I phone her on her birthday and on Christmas Day) has always thought it strange that I was the only one who addressed her by her maiden name.) On this occasion she said the beehive in my grandad's back garden had somehow fallen over and the bees were all over the place, so until it was back to normal I had to wait at her home. I can remember when the honey combs were taken out. We'd be given a piece and chew it until all the honey had been eaten.

The first half of our property consisted of the house and then the garage with two rooms attached. The other half was what I'd call the orchard. There were mango trees, avocados, guavas, lemons and many other fruit trees. This was all fenced in and this is where I also kept all my chickens. I made nests all around. There were wooden ramps at the bottom of some of the trees. The chickens all slept in the trees. There were no chicken houses at all. If ever chickens were described as free range then these would be top of the list. Occasionally one or two of the lightweight ones would fly over the wire netting. I'd have to then catch them and trim one of their wings, which prevented them from reaching the top of the fence.

About two miles from where we lived the area had become industrialised. There was one factory called the Bitumen factory and another called Euzol. In between these two was a small building. My grandad owned it. It was a tearoom or eating house which was used mainly by the workers who worked in the factories nearby. My aunts took it in turn to help out there.

One day my Aunt Peggy set off to go there and I wanted to go with her as well, but she said no, not on this occasion. I waited a little while and then started following her. I had to pass through this field where cattle were grazing. Because I'd always been around my grandad's cattle I wasn't afraid of them. One decided she didn't like my face and before I knew it I was being tossed in the air. My aunt heard my screams and came running back. She took me home and said she hoped I'd learnt a lesson. For years I had these two marks on my chest where the horns had grazed me, but I never ever followed my aunt again. Last year, when I phoned her on her birthday (she still has all her faculties and her hearing is OK), I reminded her about that incident. She was amazed that I still remembered it. The Euzol factory next to the tearoom used bottles for something or other and we'd collect any that were clear of any printing and we'd earn a few pennies.

One night there was a burglary at my grandad's house. They didn't catch the burglar, but there were clothes and other things strewn all over the grass. When I wanted to know how he'd got away – I suppose because I was so inquisitive – they said he'd been naked and covered in oil and they called him Slippery Jim. Of course, I believed them.

Not long after this happened I had to go into hospital to have my tonsils removed. My sister had had hers removed and she was back home within three days, so it was expected that I would be the same. But being me, I developed a cold or some other infection so they didn't operate until I was better. In the meantime, the children's ward was full so I was put into a ward with grown-ups.

They started chatting to me to make me feel comfortable and I told them all about 'Slippery Jim', which they found amusing.

But that night I really became ill and started hallucinating. I jumped out of bed and started running out of the ward shouting to everyone to catch 'Slippery Jim'. Well, they caught me instead and took me back to the ward and gave me something to calm me down. The next day when my mum and aunts visited they were told what had happened. I think I was nine at the time and felt really foolish. Strangely enough, I can still see the clothes all strewn on the grass, as though it were yesterday.

At one time during my childhood my parents were going through a bad patch financially. We always made our own bread. We'd get sent to the shop to buy flour. The bags had 'Blue Ribbon Flour Mills' printed on them. My mum would boil this material (I don't know how many times) until the print had vanished; she'd then make us short-sleeved shirts and shorts.

When we played cowboys and crooks we'd carve out our guns from pieces of wood. I was always Ken Maynard – the others had names such as Gary Cooper, Buck Jones, Roy Rogers etc. Up on the hill above Dennis' house there were these three mango trees. Here the game was cops and robbers. One day I landed on a dead branch and fell to the ground. I was knocked out for a little while and had a slight headache. Other than that I was fine. Ever since that happened, to the present time, I can't stand heights.

Further along from these trees there were some avocado trees. A distance away was this large forbidding-looking house. Apparently a Mrs Jacobs lived there (was the area named after her?), but no one had ever seen her. Also, we were told that she had this huge African who looked after her property. He was said to carry a gun loaded with pepper. We'd believe anything we were told, a whole load of rubbish. In any case Africans weren't even allowed to possess guns.

As I was the smallest I had to stay at the bottom of the trees and keep a look out for this mythical man whom we called 'Jugger'. Don't ask me where his name came from.

Suddenly, someone shouted "Jugger!". They were out of the trees in a flash, avocados falling out of shirts. I tripped as I was running, and my uncle Pat (whom I didn't call Uncle, as he was only four years older than me) grabbed hold of me and started dragging me down. I was bruised all over. Of course we never ever saw "Jugger". I wonder if he was just a figment of our imagination.

At the bottom of the hill below Dennis' house there was a small cemetery which had the graves of Afrikaner soldiers who had fought the British. There were small headstones showing each grave with a monument in the centre with the names of those who had died. The Afrikaners were going to celebrate a special date in their history and it was going to be where we lived. A road was renamed 'Voortrekker Street', and houses and land were being bought up by the Afrikaners.

My grandad, who still worked for the big property people, was engaged in building the roads and selling the plots of land. This is how the Gunters came to meet him, and they bought his home (where Slippery Jim had been) as well as the smaller one which was next to ours. My grandad then moved into my other aunt's house, which was on the other side.

Voortrekker Cemetary

It was a day I remember; more a week, I think. The Afrikaners came from all over, dressed in clothes similar to the ones they wore in bygone days, the women in long frilly dresses and big bonnets, the men with large hats and big beards. There were the wagons being pulled by long-horned oxen.

The new neighbours, the Gunters (pronounced with a soft 'g'), were very involved. The family were all huge in build, five sons and one daughter. They let it be known they were of pure German ancestry, and could hardly speak a word of English (not that they were keen to). But in the 16 or so years they lived next door to us, their English did improve whereas our Afrikaans, not a jot. I could never ever hold a conversation in the language.

It was amazing how well we got on together considering the way they were brought up, never to mix with anyone (black or white) except Afrikaners. But then in those days there was no such thing as Apartheid. The word hadn't been invented. People married whom they liked and lived where they liked, even if it was frowned upon by some, although in the city there were laws separating the different race groups. It was probably true to say that half of South African whites had a certain amount of colour in their DNA – what we used to call "a touch of the tar brush".

I would describe the area where we lived as grey. There were families who were white, white families who had maternal grandmothers who were of mixed blood, and then there was my grandfather who'd married a black woman. Actually, she was the only black. Playing with the Gunter boys – Christian and Hendrick and Sucky – it never entered my head that I was of mixed blood. I was just me.

One day my grandad wanted me to take him into the city on business. Normally he went everywhere by car, but there was a problem with the car. He'd never been on a bus in his life, so this was a new experience for him.

So off into town we went, sitting downstairs in the bus, which was for whites only. On our way at one of the bus stops waiting to get on was Mrs Edwards.

Mrs Edwards lived in a beautiful house in our area and she knew my grandad quite well. She was always well-dressed, wearing gloves as well as a huge hat, and whenever I saw pictures of our Queen Mum it always reminded me of Mrs Edwards. She was slightly deaf and spoke loudly and you'd also have to speak loud for her to hear you.

Big Daddy

As soon as she saw my grandad it was "Hello Albert". I had to get out of my seat for her to sit next to him. Of course they were talking quite loudly and perhaps because they didn't want other passengers to hear what they were saying, they started speaking in the African language in which they were both fluent. The rest of the whites couldn't believe what they were hearing: two white people speaking Zulu or Xhosa (I'm not sure which).

Another time, all school children were invited to Boswells Circus which was performing in town. Years before, there was a well-known lady who ran a very high class 'Shebeen'. The laws being what they were, there were strict times when liquor could be bought and bars open, so Mrs Dry catered for the wealthy people who wanted a drink whenever. At one time, the officials were so exasperated with her that she was banned from town but after a couple of years she returned.

At the circus this magician was telling everyone how he went for a drink at Mrs Dry's. He was going to make the drink disappear, which it did. I felt like jumping up and saying I knew her personally because she was the midwife at my birth and she was Mrs Edwards' sister, but of course I didn't dare.

I became much closer to my grandad when I started writing his business letters. Aunt Peggy used to do it, but she now had a boyfriend and Big Daddy found he couldn't really rely on her.

Whenever he was due to work for a long period he would set up camp. His cottage could be knocked up in a couple of days. He'd have his cattle there and grow vegetables. Sometimes he'd be in the same place for over a year. During the school holidays we'd spend a lot of time there. This particular time he was situated about 15 or 20 miles out of Durban. There was a river nearby where we swam and guavas grew wild. In the bushes were monkeys and, no doubt, snakes. (Which thankfully, we never saw.)

There was this guy (I think you'd call him an entrepreneur?) taking a large group of Kalahari bushmen to the cities in South Africa for the whites who had never seen bushmen to observe what they looked like (not nice at all when you think about it now). However, when he arrived in Durban he had nowhere to put them. Because the place where my grandad had his headquarters seemed ideal, he was asked if he could have them stationed there for a week. People from all over came to see them. Years later, when I was in high school, we had a lesson on the Kalahari bushmen. Our teacher was from the UK, so of course didn't know of them coming to Durban.

In fact, none of the children in my class knew about it, and when I said to the teacher they'd been at my grandad's place of work, they thought I was making it up and I felt a bit of a fool.

When I got home I asked my parents if they had any photos of the bushmen. I took these to school the next time we had a lesson on the indigenous tribes of South Africa and this time I was quite popular with my classmates. Unfortunately, because I never thought I'd be writing my story no photos were kept. I've written to people in South Africa, contacted the newspapers and city libraries and websites on Durban in the 1930s and early 1940s, but to no avail.

My original birth place

The last time I visited Durban was in 2009. The area where I was born is now unrecognisable from how it used to be. There is now a huge factory on the exact spot where our home was. I even contacted the owners to see if they had any photos of the area before the factory was built, but they couldn't help. Where the Afrikaner cemetery is I just saw the monument with railings around it with factories on either side. So far no one wants to dig up the graves and develop it. I doubt if modern day Afrikaners know of its history. I caught a bus that went along Chamberlain Road with factories on either side and then reached the Bitumen factory which is now long gone, and there between the factories was this small rusty-looking cottage that I'm sure was my grandad's eating house. It was obviously unoccupied. Recently I looked at the area on Google, but the little cottage wasn't there.

My one regret is that although I have all the pictures as clear as anything in my mind I am unable to share them with anyone.

There were five of us in our family. My brother Arthur, me, my younger sister Inez – whom everyone called Pinky (she hated the name Inez but had to endure being called it at school) – then Glen and Redvers (Reds) the youngest.

The Riots in 1949

Top of the list for visitors to Durban was the Indian Market. It was situated in the heart of the city and people from all over shopped there, especially on Saturdays. The bus rank, which comprised many buses, took passengers to all areas of the town. Even though the Indians had no political clout, they just went about their lives making money. They owned bioscopes, huge furniture stores, and, it was said, a third of Durban. The natives (Africans), meanwhile, were very poor and many worked as servants for the wealthy Indians. Inwardly they resented them, and in 1949 (January, I think), they turned on them and rioted. I'm not sure but I think an Indian bus knocked over an African and this was just what was needed to start the riot.

Everyone was told to get home before dark and Indian workers were told to stay overnight in their places of work. Because I went to work by bike my Dad phoned the firm and told me he'd pick me up by car. The Indians living around our area all went to a place of safety, except for the old Indian everyone called 'Punchum'.

I knew him from when I was a youngster. He owned a few cattle, grew mealies (maize) and other vegetables, which he went around selling. We'd go there early in the morning to collect milk and occasionally while they were doing the milking we'd have a go, and being small, we were able to squeeze the udders and the warm milk would go into our throats. I still have that taste when I drink milk.

Punchum said he'd lived there most of his life and wasn't leaving his home and cattle, and no one harmed him. What I remember most about Punchum was that he was always dressed in white robes and his hair was swept up into a long plait, just like Ghandi. He was timeless and still alive when I left South Africa in 1956.

Starting work

I would have liked to have furthered my education having started my matriculation. Up until then, education had been free, but now a pupil's family would be assessed to see if they could afford to pay the fees. My father didn't think he could, so I had to leave school, but before I left our teacher wanted to know what some of us wanted to be in later life. Of course, my dream was to become a poultry farmer. Very far-fetched I must admit.

My dad had a friend who worked in a car showroom that had a garage attached. He arranged for me to start working there. I was never interested in cars anyway, but did as I was told. I kept asking my boss when was I going to sign the apprenticeship papers and he was always making excuses. Little did I know at the time that, having left school at the age of sixteen and having had a happy life I was leaving it behind, and unknown to me the seed was being sown that would change my life completely.

I realised later than it was the fact that I was mixed race, and that only whites were given apprenticeships. The worst thing was that a white youngster who hadn't even passed his standard six exam was given one ahead of me, but my boss was put in an awkward situation not of his doing. He arranged with a business friend of his to employ me as a panel beater.

While working in the garage there was this friend of my boss who visited quite frequently. His name was Ashley Clive Smith. I'd never heard the name 'Ashley' before and thought then that if I ever had a son he'd be called Ashley. When our son was born, Olive was quite happy for him to be called Ashley.

Although still not crazy about cars I was happier panel beating. I worked with the guy who repaired radiators, welded and repaired bumpers – petrol tanks, exhaust pipes, stainless steel, brass and other metals. He, Mr Watson, eventually left to settle in the UK, and I took over from him, being the only one who did that job. I still wasn't interested in cars and couldn't even drive. I rode my bike the seven miles to work every day.

The boys in the area decided to form a band. I was 16 at the time. Dennis, who I grew up with, could play most instruments including the piano, guitar, trumpet, and bass. Yes, very talented, our Dennis. I could play the piano but not very well. I preferred dancing to the music. We'd hire halls in small towns in the Transkei, collect entrance fees at the door, and that way we were able to buy all the instruments we needed for the band like drums and saxophone. We called ourselves Gay Caballeros, with Mexican hats and red neckties. One of our favourite songs when we got together was called "Durban is the place for me". It was our signature tune played and sung with a samba beat and went well with our name. Even here in the UK when we sang it at a party it went down well with Dennis playing the piano and Peter playing the guitar. I don't know who composed or introduced it or how it came about but these are the words.

Durban this is the place for me
Durban I love you so
Kimberley is very nice to see
Jo'burg is pretty
And so is Capetown City
But it's Durban
That is the place for me
It's tropical climate suits me to a T
You can go to Swaziland
Somaliland is full of sand
But Durban is the place for me

Chorus

You can cruise around the bay
Just to while the time away
Or walk along the palm -fringed Esplanade
You can watch the silvery moon
Shine upon the Blue Lagoon
So come and spend this life with me.

I think at times like that we did tend to feel a little homesick.

Of course, breeding chickens and keeping pets were being left by the wayside.

I had known Olive when she'd been to Durban visiting, but got to know her better when we went to Flagstaff where she was originally from. Whenever we were in Flagstaff we'd meet up and when she came to Durban as well.

Becoming a father

Olive came down to Durban quite often and we were very much in love. It wasn't long after Christmas 1950 she said she was pregnant. What were we thinking? Her mother was in Durban. Her brother, much older and nearer my parents' age, came down from Flagstaff to try to sort out what these 'children' had done. I was not yet 20 and Olive was 16. Olive and I were in love and there was only one answer to that. We were married within a month. At the rear of our house there was a massive garage with two rooms attached and my parents said we could start our married life there. We were very fortunate as I was still an apprentice and not earning very much.

Olive had been born with a club foot, but when I was a teenager the only way you'd know she had a disability was the slight limp she had, as her left leg was a tiny bit shorter. But she could run, jump and dance, and most of her friends were unaware of any disability. In the cold winter months she'd feel a pain on her left side.

Just before we married my dad mentioned this to me, and asked if I realised in the future she might need medical care. I told him that in her life someone would fall in love with her and want to marry her, and that someone just turned out to be me. He never ever mentioned it again. Throughout her pregnancy I worried that our baby might be born like that, although Olive wasn't concerned at all.

At the hospital they said it would be a long while before she gave birth and that I should go home. The next morning my grandad had a phone call saying Olive had given birth to a boy (he was the only one in our road who had a phone). He was getting annoyed at me because I kept asking if they'd said anything else. When I got to the hospital the first thing I looked at were his legs. After all these months I could now relax. I had become paranoid with worry and what my dad had said hadn't helped.

Olive did say during labour that her leg went completely dead, yet strangely enough, ever since she's never suffered with pain in the winter. We had a scare when Ashley started to walk – the doctors said his ankles needed strengthening. I remember buying him tiny boots, and ever since then he's been fine.

Tragedy (My brother's suicide)

Arthur was always in some sort of trouble. I remember one Saturday morning, my dad had gone to work and Mum had gone shopping. Arthur turned up with some of his mates and demanded that my sister cooked them a meal. She refused and I sided with her. It was just before he joined the army so he was 16 at the time. I was 12. By now his friends were out of the house by the front gate and Arthur was threatening to hit me. Of course, I couldn't stand up to him. But there happened to be a bicycle wheel nearby on the verandah. I grabbed hold of it and held it in front of me for protection.

In the meantime my brother Glen had run to call my grandmother, 'Tuku Mama', and when Arthur saw her he retreated with his mates.

When he came back from the war and reverted to his former lifestyle with drink and drugs, the only person he'd listen to was Mrs Van der Byl, Dennis and Peter's mum. She would speak to him and calm him down. It is ironic that when he committed suicide the first people we sought out were Dennis' family and a week after the funeral we were woken up by Dennis and his brother saying their mum had passed away. She'd had an asthma attack and had died instantly. She was still in her forties and Alvin, the youngest, was only four years old. So the following week, the same people in the community, plus the Van der Byl family relatives, were at the funeral. Yes, our families do have a lot in common, with Arthur and Mrs Van dying within a fortnight of each other, and years later Peter and I leaving the country together.

He was a problem for my parents because of the company he kept, and he was always getting into trouble. He had joined the army when he was 16 but rather than tell the authorities he was underage, they decided it might be the making of him. He served in Italy and North Africa and when he returned he was a bit of a hero and quite popular with the girls. But it wasn't long before he reverted to his old ways mixing with riffraff who smoked dugga (marijuana). My parents were at their wits' end not knowing what to do next after he'd been in a brawl and lost an eye.

Olive was six months pregnant as this time. She saw him sitting under a tree writing a letter. She asked him who he was writing it to and he said a friend he'd recently met.

Our house was built on high foundations with huge arched openings which allowed air to circulate. If one of the hens made a nest there I'd usually get in to collect the eggs. It just shows how roomy it was. Above one of these openings was my sister's bedroom. Unknown to my parents, my brother had somehow found the key to the locked wardrobe in which the guns were kept. He'd stolen the shotgun and hidden it under my sister's bedroom. It was just after midnight when there was a loud banging on our bedroom door. My father and sister were saying Arthur had shot himself. I ran into the house and into the room where he was lying, already dead.

Apparently when he'd returned home he'd retrieved the gun, went into the bedroom he shared with my two younger brothers, Glen and Redvers, and gave Glen the letter he'd written earlier. Glen ran to call my mum and as she came into the room she saw the gun at the side of his head, she shouted to him not to do it but he just said "I'm sorry, Mum" and pulled the trigger right in front of her.

My mum was a very strong woman and had had her kidney removed when I was fifteen. How she got through the next few days I'll never know. It was a night I'll never forget. The police were called. Fortunately the police sergeant knew my family and when they found my brother had drugs on him they did not inform the media. So at least my parents were freed that humiliation.

Break-up

After Ashley was born, Olive and I rented the house next door. This was the house owned by the Duncans, the Gunters' in-laws. They in turn sold it to a Mr Briggs who had emigrated from London. It was his second house and we rented it from him.

Originally when my grandad built it for his daughter – my Aunt Vi – it was going to be part of a bigger house which never happened. It was quite small – bedroom, lounge, bathroom and kitchen – but it suited us fine and at first we were very happy. Olive took a job at the Lion match factory. She said it would help us financially, which it did. We had an African maid who came in in the morning and left in the afternoon. It wasn't a problem as my parents were next door if she needed any help. The Lion match employed women who were white and any who passed as white, and no questions asked. Except for Olive's mother who was of mixed parentage her family were white and in Durban they wouldn't encounter any problems. In their small town of Flagstaff it was a different matter altogether.

It was at this time that Olive's brother Bertram – who was nearer my mother's age, and whom I'd had to give up my bed for when he brought Pondo workers from the Transkei to Durban – that would be a 300 mile drive and he'd stay overnight at our home before heading back to Flagstaff (I mention this to show how close he was to our family) – came to Durban with his wife and children to settle permanently. And not once did he come to see my mum and dad, let alone his sister and Ashley whom he never ever saw.

Olive would visit them sometimes, going straight from work. Of course now they were completely white. In fact, from that day Mrs Wardell, Olive's mother, never ever saw her grandchildren again. Olive would never admit it, but I think she was told by her brother she'd have to decide which side of the fence she was going to be on because now, no one knew the family background. They were in a white area with the children in a white school. We'd had a silly argument about a dress she wanted to buy and I said she really didn't need it. She then said she was leaving. Not taking it seriously I said, "Go, but don't take Ashley." I think that was music to her ears, because she just packed a bag, didn't even look at her son, and walked out. I fully expected her to return but she never did.

At first she lodged with a family she knew. I'd see her when she caught a bus to work and tried to get her to come home, but I gave up in the end. She'd made up her mind from then on that she was white, and never mixed with anyone she'd known previously.

She came back again to fetch a few more of her things. After we divorced, she met up with an Italian immigrant much older than herself. They had a son. Her family doesn't know anything of her former life and don't even know of Ashley's existence.

After Olive left I lived on my own with Ashley. The African maid would come in the morning and then I'd leave for work. She'd cook and bathe Ashley and leave when I returned. If there was a problem (luckily none occurred) my mum and dad were next door. After a year in this situation my parents said I could come back home, which I did.

Bertram (Olive's brother) in the meantime had a job working for Coedmore Quarries and in the field opposite our home the firm was removing soil, and Bertram was driving the tipper truck.

When I came home my mum said Ashley was fascinated watching it from the kitchen window, of course not knowing it was his uncle who was driving it. Even though there was no one in the vicinity who might have seen him (and even if they did would not have noticed), he didn't even come over to say hello to my mum or see Ashley – and this was the man for whom I had given up my bed for when he travelled down to Durban, and my parents who had known him and his family all their lives. How sad.

Deciding to leave

I can remember the time when the film 'Carmen Jones' was going to be shown in Durban. It was only going to be screened at one of the city's main cinemas. At these cinemas – the Metro-20th Century Fox – cinema goers really dressed for the occasion, unlike the smaller ones. Anyway, 'Carmen Jones' wasn't going to be shown in any non-white cinemas because it showed American blacks drinking, and blacks in South Africa were only allowed to drink their own kaffir beer. Of course I wanted to see the film but wasn't quite sure whether I'd be able to buy a ticket. So I wrote a note for two of the expensive seats and sent my African assistant to get it. My aunt, who could pass for white, went with me and we both enjoyed the film. Another time, Billy – Dennis' brother – and I went to the Princes Cinema and decided to go for a drink. Billy only drank Cane spirits which was only sold in non-white bars, so even though we were dressed to the nines we walked into the non-white bar with everyone staring at us. One minute we were trying to be white, the next quite happy to be non-white.

Once I realised that Ashley had a white half-brother, I knew I couldn't live with the knowledge that he would be inferior and how it might affect him in later years, especially living in the same city. But how to go about it?

My sister's in-laws had been to the UK for a holiday, and when they returned her father-in-law threw a party and invited the crew who had looked after them. A few were from Southampton and I got chatting to them, and they said quite frequently Union Castle employed crew from Durban.

I'd get on my bike during my lunch break when one of the Union Castle ships was in port and enquire about a job, but I was always told they only needed experienced silver service hands. I only realised much later that the South African policy was whites only and because they weren't quite sure where they stood with me and my situation they decided to take the easy way out. What if I'd gone with my grandad? Who knows what might have happened? So that was another route closed to me.

Charlie Moodie was born in Newcastle and had gone out to South Africa as a teenager. He met his wife Muriel whom I'd known most of my life. My description of her is she was white. Not quite there but passable. They married and had two girls. Charlie was an experienced mechanic and was also into racing cars. He was in the process of building his own car and asked me to help with the welding. They then decided they'd sell the car and emigrate to the UK, settling in Kent.

When I told them I wanted to leave South Africa it was decided we'd go together. I started saving like mad. I was going to go to Earl's Court in London where all South Africans, Australians and New Zealanders went. I didn't have a clue really but the seed had been sown. Our plans were coming along fine. Charlie's car was completed and once he had sold it we would be booking our tickets. I couldn't wait for it to happen.

I came home from work a couple of days later. My brother Glen said he had some news for me, news I wasn't going to like hearing. Charlie, Muriel and their daughters had left for Rhodesia with the car. I couldn't believe it. Not a word to me and I'd spoken to them two days before. I was really knocked for six. I was at the stage now where I couldn't give up.

The Van der Byl family and ours were very close. Dennis, who is my age and who now lives in Leicester, came a year after Peter and I. Peter was much younger. He used to come over to where I worked during his and my lunch hour. He was also disillusioned with life in South Africa. He was eager to leave with me but didn't have enough saved, and as he was eighteen he'd need his father's consent. I said I'd help him with the fare and would speak to his dad about giving his consent.

His father was quite happy to give his consent. Everyone thought we were mad, going to a country where we didn't know anyone, and all my father said was, "Do you know the price of liquor and the cost of cigarettes?" That definitely wasn't a vote of confidence.

At last the day arrived. We were sailing on the Arundel Castle, Peter and I with our suitcases, off into the unknown, but desperate to get away. The majority of people we knew seemed content with their lives in South Africa, but for us it wasn't so.

Ashley was six years old and I was leaving him with my mum and dad. I knew then that somehow I'd return one day to bring him to the UK, but I also knew I'd never return to live in South Africa.

As the ship left the Port of Durban I felt a lump in my throat seeing family and friends waving goodbye to Peter and me. We soon hit the open sea and the ship started listing, first to the left and then to the right. Having never sailed before we felt seasick and made our way to our cabin. It was situated below deck with no porthole and just above the propellers. I wondered how on earth we were going to endure the noise for a fortnight but with the continuous noise it soon lulled us into a peaceful sleep. We awoke after a couple of hours and feeling hungry went up to the dining room, but it was deserted. The passengers had already eaten and left. A kind steward made us some sandwiches.

We arrived in Cape Town and were there for four days while the ship loaded cargo for the UK. Peter's brother Dennis had already left Durban and was living in Cape Town. He was employed at

Cape Town's top restaurant 'The Waldorf' as a pianist and vocalist. Peter and I were invited as his personal guests and I was surprised at how well he could sing, sort of Frank Sinatra.

Becoming British

We arrived a fortnight later on a Thursday morning in Southampton. We'd made friends with one of the deck hands who said he'd show us around Southampton before we left for London. We realised by late afternoon that he wasn't going to turn up, and we weren't too keen on going to London so late in the day. What on earth were we thinking? We really didn't have a clue. Earl's Court was just a name. Would we even know how to get there?

Peter suddenly said there was a family friend who lived in Southampton but he didn't know the address. We went to the Guild Hall to enquire. Maybe it was the electoral register – I don't recall now – but we did obtain the address. Luckily it wasn't far from the city centre. We caught a bus, leaving our suitcases at the left luggage locker at the railway station. How lucky we were. Pat Diedericks, the family friend, was a steward on the Queen Mary and was home on two weeks' leave. We have a lot to thank him for. He told us we were crazy to even think of going to London without any plans.

He and his wife said we should stay there while we decided what to do. They had the local paper. I looked at the vacancy job section and saw a firm wanted a radiator repairer. The next day (Friday), I went for an interview and they said I could start on the Monday. I told Peter to start looking for digs, and we were on our way. That was in October 1956.

Pat and his wife and three sons spent Christmas at her family's home in Southend. My employer's mother and daughter invited Peter and I to spend Christmas with their family. We were ever so pleased as we didn't know anyone else. Actually on Christmas morning we woke up to see everything covered in snow. We were like two children never having seen snow before. Peter had worked for a cycle firm in Durban and got a job at Halfords, so we were now OK financially.

A week after arriving in Southampton Peter and I decided to go to London to check out Earl's Court. Somehow or other we found ourselves in Trafalgar Square. There were thousands of people carrying placards saying "Eden must go". We hadn't realised it was the time of the Suez Crisis. We had to make sure we didn't get separated. We did see a big black guy arm-in-arm with a white blonde woman, and I said to Peter, "If Dr Malan or Verwoerd saw this they'd commit suicide." We never did get to see what Earl's Court was like.

I wasted no time in applying for a British passport, which I got without a problem as my dad was British before the South African government took over from the British.

Derek Nicholson also lodged where Peter and I stayed. He was a New Zealander from Auckland and had been in the UK for a couple of years. He was older than Peter but younger than me. So the three of us went out to pubs, dancing, swimming, and life was good.

At one of the dance halls I frequented I met Joan, and we fell in love. Derek was a carpenter and when he took his annual holiday decided to drive up to Scotland. I wondered whether his Morris Minor would take him there and back but he assured us it was quite roadworthy. I suddenly remembered John MacBean, the sailor who used to visit our house during the war when I was eleven. I asked Derek, when he got to Inverness, to enquire at the local swimming baths if they remembered a John MacBean who worked there before the war. Well, Derek saw this guy there and asked him. And he said, "Actually, I'm John MacBean."

Then Derek explained the reason he'd asked. When Derek returned he told me all about it and gave me John's address. I was flabbergasted. We started corresponding. I eventually went to Inverness, met his wife Margaret and his family of two grown-up children and had a wonderful time up there.

It's all such a long time ago now, but the time I spent visiting John in Inverness was really enjoyable. When I arrived in Inverness I decided to stay at a bed and breakfast a stone's throw away from where he lived. He and his family made me feel ever so welcome.

What surprised him was that I'd remembered what he'd said to me about working in the swimming baths and living in Inverness, and also the name of his ship because I was only 11 at the time. Whether it was the war and what it can do to a young serviceman's mind, I don't know, but he seemed reluctant to recall things at that time. Even his friend Alan Whitehead didn't seem to ring a bell. I remember Alan gave my cousin Garner his knife and John gave me his. Their names were engraved on them. Maybe they themselves hadn't been friends for long, because Alan left the base first. War can do awful things to one's life.

That evening John said he was going to entertain me and he certainly did. I was taken to meet his friends and of course we visited pubs. He was telling his friends about the pets I kept – chickens, rabbits and even the little deer I called 'Sally'. Of course his friends insisted I have a wee dram. I wasn't partial to the taste of Scotch and said only if I was allowed to add a dash of lemon. John was a true Scot and was eager to show me as much of Inverness as he could in the short time I was up there. He'd finished at the swimming baths and was manager at the market. This gave him time to show me places of interest.

Loch Ness. Now that was a visit I shall not forget. It was in the morning. It was misty and looking over the water I could just imagine the Loch Ness Monster appearing. I also visited the ancient battlefield monument and other places of interest. Sadly many of the names I can't recall. There was no let up. It was a week full of entertainment. So thank you, John and Margaret, I had a wonderful week in Inverness.

By now Dennis had arrived in the UK and was living in London, singing and playing in a band at the Café de Paris. Peter visited him a lot and said he was thinking of living there as well. Being with his brother would be ideal.

Joining the Merchant Navy

Derek was becoming home-sick and so was I, missing Ashley more than anything else. One day, Derek turned up at my place of work and went into the office. I don't know what he said, but he came out and said I had the afternoon off. Something to do with my family.

We went straight down to the 'pool'; that is where they recruited for the Merchant Navy. He said he was a carpenter and I said I was a panel beater. After a while they told us to come back the following week with our suitcases, ready to sail. I gave in my notice. They were sorry I was leaving but when I explained the real reason they understood. We thought they'd put us on the same ship, but they put Derek on a cargo ship going to South America, as the ship's chippy (carpenter).

I was put on the Queen Elizabeth. I was in a cabin with six other guys who were from all over the UK. They, like me, were all first-timers. My job was cleaning out the bilges. If I could have got off the ship I would have. I thought, "What have I got myself into?!" Cleaning the bilges was one of the worst jobs ever.

However, after five days of sailing and seeing the lights of New York as we approached the port, I thought to myself, for someone coming from Jacobs, finding myself here in New York was unbelievable. The ship would usually stay a day in Southampton and then turn around. I did four trips, getting promoted to fireman, then to greaser. The next time in Southampton I saw that the Arundel Castle would be leaving the following week for South Africa. I went down to the pool (shipping federation) to see if there were any vacancies but was told she was fully crewed up. Of course the guys working for Union Castle company knew South Africa's policy on recruiting whites only.

So once again I got on my bike and rode down to the ship where they were signing on. I saw the guy who was in charge of taking on engine room ratings and he told me to hang about. After about an hour he came to me and said there was a job going, gave me a paper to fill in, and told me to take it back to the federation. If looks could have killed I'd have been dead on the spot. It was the same guy who'd told me there weren't any vacancies, and I hadn't just got on my bike and gone home, but defied him by going to see for myself. After that, with one signing in my discharge book on a Union Castle ship I encountered no further problems getting on any other Union Castle ship. One thing I noticed, there were never any non-whites employed. I don't think I stood out though. The Arundel Castle was the ship I'd come over on as a passenger and now I was going back on the same ship as a crew member.

The ship arrived in Durban on the Christmas weekend. The chief engineer gave me time off, and the family were overjoyed to see me. I hadn't told them I was coming, so it was good to see the happy smiles on their faces when I turned up.

Especially Ashley. He was shy at first, but soon we were great together, and once he knew I'd be returning every six weeks, everything was good.

Derek in the meantime had met a girl in Argentina who asked him to give a parcel to a cousin in London who was a nurse. Derek fell in love with the nurse and went back to New Zealand with her and they married there.

Joan and I married in 1961 and since I was still in the Merchant Navy her parents said we should stay with them until we decided our future. It would allow us to save as well. Whenever I arrived back I'd have loads of fruit – pineapples, oranges, tomatoes and bananas from the Canaries – and sheer nylon stockings for Joan, because at that time they were scarce and also expensive.

A couple of years later I worked on a Shaw Savill cargo ship which went to Australia and New Zealand. When we arrived in Auckland I decided to look Derek up. We hadn't been corresponding and I didn't have an address. I looked in the phone book but there were quite a few Nicholsons. After trying a few numbers I got lucky. This guy said he knew a Derek Nicholson who worked building yachts. Remembering that Derek was a carpenter, I went to the address and sure enough there was Derek. We were both made up to see each other. I told him I'd married Joan. He'd known her when he lived in Southampton. He insisted I met his family. By now he was a father of two sons. We were there for two weeks and he and his wife showed me so much of the area that I fell in love with the place and I thought it was a country I'd like to emigrate to; that is, if I could persuade Joan.

When I returned to the UK, I mentioned it to Joan, but she wasn't enthusiastic at all. I told her I'd give up the sea, find work ashore and look for a place of our own. She was adamant she wasn't going to move out of her parents' home. I just couldn't understand it.

About eighteen months later I did another trip to New Zealand with the ship calling at Durban on the way back. By now, Derek had four sons and I asked him how many more they were going to have. All he said was "She's Roman Catholic"!

Joan's one excuse was that she wouldn't emigrate to a country not knowing how we'd earn a living and where we'd live. I went for an interview for a panel beating job and was told it would be kept open for me should I decide to emigrate to the country, and Derek and his wife were happy to sponsor us, and housing wouldn't be a problem.

I wrote to Joan telling her all this and she wrote back saying she would not be leaving her parents' home under any circumstances. I knew then that my marriage was not going to last.

Bringing Ashley to Britain

On the way back, sailing towards Durban, I thought about my future and realised that not only losing Joan, but if I wasn't careful I'd lose Ashley as well. When we arrived in Durban I asked my mum if I could take Ashley to live with me in the UK. He was thirteen and had still never seen his mother who lived in the same city. I knew it would break my mum's heart to let him leave but she knew he'd have a better life in England. She made me promise that I'd bring him back to visit. I made that promise because at the back of my mind I had plans which I would strive to make happen.

Young Ashley

Peter's youngest brother Alvin was four years older than Ashley and when I told Peter I was bringing Ashley he said he'd like Alvin to come as well. I was pleased about that as they'd grown up together and they'd be company for each other in a new country.

On arrival back in the UK I left the Merchant Navy. I didn't go back to Joan. Her twin brother and his wife said I could stay with them, but not wanting them involved I declined. I lived in digs, and was looking for a flat, then found one and flew the boys over. Peter didn't have room for Alvin in London so he came to Southampton and lived with Ashley and I. Alvin found work in the big department store Edwin Jones and Ashley started school. Before they'd arrived I'd furnished the flat with some second-hand furniture and went to the local market to buy pots, pans, curtains, sheets, you name it, everything I thought that was needed.

It was a ground floor flat in a detached house. It had a large living room, one bedroom, a small dining room, a kitchen and a bathroom. The boys shared the bedroom and I used the living room as my bedroom.

Joan started visiting us. In fact, she quite liked Ashley and he called her Aunt. She managed a cake shop and when he passed it on his way to school with his friend she'd call him and give them some cakes. But she would never stay with me at the flat, always going back to her parents' home. Even Ashley started asking what was going on. The next time she came I asked her to decide what she was going to do. She said she was sorry but she was staying with her parents. That was the end of my marriage.

When friends asked the reasons for the break-up, I said I didn't understand, but deep down I knew why.

Needless to say I really loved Joan, and it took me a long time to get her out of my system. I'd lie awake at night for hours, unable to sleep. But I had a son to raise and work to get to. This all happened in 1964.

It must have been in 1965, anyway, Ashley was still at school. It was a Saturday, and he'd gone to play football. I was waiting for him to come home. I'd just made a meal and I was going out that evening dancing at the Royal Pier, which was one of the places to go to on a Saturday night. And I really loved dancing.

The door opened. Ashley came in, and who should walk in behind him? Charlie Moodie, Muriel and their two daughters. I'd last seen them when Ashley was six years old and now he was fifteen. These were the people, once my friends, who'd left Durban for Rhodesia without even saying goodbye.

Apparently they'd got my address from Peter's sister, flown to Heathrow, got a train to Southampton, left their luggage at the station, and came looking for me. They happened to see Ashley at the bus stop and recognised him.

Could they spend the night at my place? They were looking at one of those static caravans at a park the next morning and would I take them there? That was the night my life changed forever. I never did go to the Royal Pier that night, and not for a long while after that. And coward that I was, I didn't have the guts to ask them how they had the nerve to come to me asking for my help after they'd treated me the way they had.

The next day on the way to the park, we passed a car showroom that had a Jaguar there. Margaret, the older daughter, said in her posh private school accent, "Oh look, Daddy, there's a car just like ours!" I thought to myself, "If they're thinking of Jaguars they can't be short of money, and I'll soon be rid of them."

In the end they found the caravan unsuitable. The suitcases were collected from the station and they were looking for a flat to rent, which proved impossible because most wouldn't allow pets or children. I put them in my bedroom and moved in with Ashley.

Dennis, Alvin, Val and Peter

Fulfilling a promise

Ashley was now beginning to ask questions about Olive and the reasons we broke up. He knew nothing of the colour problem in South Africa and how it had been the cause of our marriage break-up. He wondered if maybe I'd ill-treated her in some way.

Also unknown to me Charlie had written to his mother-in-law telling her to come over. So the next thing was Muriel's mother arriving. This was just too much. I needed to do something, and fast. I had a chat with Ashley telling him of my plans. By now he was sixteen and had left school. I went down to the shipping federation and said I'd like my son to become a seaman. There was no way I wanted him in the engine room. They sent him to the seaman's school at Gravesend.

When he came back I'd already looked at different ships' itineraries and realised Shaw Savill's two passenger ships, the 'Southern Cross' and 'Northern Star' were each sailing to Australia and New Zealand, calling at Durban and Cape Town. One was going through the Suez Canal and the other through the Panama Canal, and that the Northern Star would be arriving in Durban two weeks before the Southern Cross. Was this luck or fate? I don't know, but I got a job on the Northern Star and got Ashley a job on the Southern Cross as an able seaman.

When I arrived in Durban I contacted Olive and said her son wanted to see her. Straight away, she said it would be impossible and I told her that if she didn't meet him he'd come knocking on her door and she'd really be in trouble explaining her double life to her white family who didn't even know Ashley existed. She quickly changed her tune and said she'd contact my sister to arrange to bring Ashley to see her. Once he'd met her he never asked about her again.

He was pleased to see my mum, dad, brothers and sister, whom he regarded as his real family. Now that he was a British seaman he could visit South Africa whenever he liked, and my mum was so pleased that I'd kept my promise that she'd see him again. In fact, she saw him many times, and saw his children when they went out there on holiday. It was years later, in 1994, when I remarried, that I took my wife Annette – whom I'd met in 1976 and married in 1980 – her daughter Kim, Ashley and his two children Tracy and Warren for a holiday. Ashley contacted his mother. She came over to see them (her grandchildren), left after an hour, never to see them again. Ashley has met up with her a couple of times and shown her photos, but she obviously can't keep any because that part of her life is a secret. I wonder if her family will even find out about her former life. Because they've never known her, Ashley's children don't seem to wonder about it all. Whether they'll change one day and become curious I'll never know. I've spoken to her in the last year and it's like speaking to someone you once knew a long time ago. She will never ask after Ashley and his family and will never mention hers – it's as though she's completely blanked her former life out of her mind.

Buying a house

The front of my first home which I sold to Ashley

Although Ashley was now independent I still had a problem of my own. My flat was just too crowded. I had been gently pushed out. I decided to let them take over the flat, put all my furniture plus everything else I owned into storage, and I then joined the small British Rail Ships which sailed from Weymouth to the Channel Isles.

I gave up smoking and drinking and started saving every penny I could. Because I was staying on the ship permanently I could do this. On my days off I'd get the train back to Southampton, get on my bike which I left at the station and would go looking at houses for sale. When I'd saved the deposit I needed I eventually found one I liked and with the help of "the man from the Pru" with whom I had an insurance policy, applied for a mortgage. At first the building society I'd applied to for a mortgage said it wasn't enough, so then I mentioned to the solicitor that unlike other applicants for first time buyers, I already had everything I needed. He said why didn't I write to them telling them what I'd told him. This I did and pleased to say I was granted a mortgage. This letter is a copy of the original one I wrote to the building society. Would someone today, being refused a mortgage, write a letter like this? I doubt it.

In some ways regarding the Moodie saga, I was a coward. But in others I think I have an inner determination to go for what I really want and sometimes won't take no for an answer. This applies to patents for my plants, where they've been rejected by some experts, but where I have obtained breeders' rights. But more of this in the chapter on my plants.

Ashley and I now had our first real home. I'd encouraged him to save and when I thought he had enough for a deposit I said he could buy my house and I'd look for another one. This would suit both of us as we both wanted to be independent, as our social lives were quite different, and I still preferred the father-son relationship to one of brothers.

The house I liked was in the Regents Park district of Southampton, not far from the one I was selling to Ashley. That house I bought in 1968 and the one I was now buying was in 1972. I am pleased to say this is still my home.

THIS IS A COPY OF THE LETTER I WROTE TO THE
BUILDING SOCIETY.

K. Rigney.
M.V. "Moose"
Weymouth.

The Manager,
Ramsbury Building Society,
Ramsbury House,
Andover.

Dear Sir,

With reference to your letter re my application
for a mortgage. I want to thank you for considering an
advance of £3.950. I had hoped for a £3600 loan with
weekly payments of £7. I have been in touch with my
solicitor & explained my position to him. He saw no harm
in my writing to you as well. Obviously I would have
preferred seeing you personally, but we are in Weymouth
for the next few weeks & it will be difficult
getting the time off. So I shall try to explain as best
I can.

I am a non smoker (having given it up 6 months ago)
and a teetaller, & enjoy perfect health. I have no
debts whatsoever & my furniture is all paid for. This
includes everything down to pots & pans. Unlike most people
buying homes I shall not need any necessary furniture
on higher purchase. The only payments I make are on
my insurance policies which I have with the Prudential
namely £1000 with profits & £3500 for endowment policy
For the past 9 months I have banked £0 per week on average.

55

and in the last month increased it to £15 per week. This is with Barclays Bank in Portswood Southampton.

I am a skilled panelbeater & whereas I commanded a much higher basic pay working ashore I find I am much better off financially working for British Railway on their cross Channel ships as my overtime is pretty regular & my board & lodging negligible.

I know my limitations and if I thought for one moment the payments with a £3600 loan would be beyond me I would be the first to admit it. I am very keen on this particular house. If I am unsuccessful in asking you to reconsider my application it means I'd have to look for something cheaper, probably pre-war, or else continue saving for a few more months. Rhodesia friends of mine have now taken over my flat I rented, & though I still use that address the majority of my furniture is in storage. So at the moment I am without a home.

Hoping my application for a higher mortgage will be favourably considered, and the reply sent to my Weymouth address.

Thanking you

Irenan

I said

Two years after I'd moved in, I was in the front garden when this car pulled up and it was Joan. She'd driven a friend of hers home and had recognised me as she passed. I was amazed as I didn't think she could drive let alone own a car. I still couldn't drive. Of course we'd parted in 1964 and in ten years a lot can change. I invited her in, we had tea together and of course talked about our marriage. She visited me a few more times when she was dropping off her friend and I think if I'd encouraged her and been more enthusiastic about starting a relationship she would have been happy to think about it. But now after ten years had passed my feelings for her were just platonic, no love, no malice, no hate, just to be friends and let the past stay in the past.

It was years later and long after our divorce that I heard she'd met someone and moved in with him. By then, both her parents had passed away.

One day while visiting Annette's parents' grave she decided to go walkabout and came back and said she'd seen Joan's parents' grave and pointed it out to me. I'd told her all about my time with Joan.

After Annette passed away I would still occasionally visit the cemetery. It was in January 2012. While there, I noticed two people at Joan's parents' grave. I realised it was Joan and probably her partner. For a minute or two I wondered whether I should approach them and how they might react. She might not have mentioned me to him.

I decided to go for it when I saw her leave him to go to a tap to fill a bottle of water for the flowers they had brought. As I approached I said, "Hello Joan." She looked at me and said, "Do I know you?" I said, "I'm Ken." She threw her arms around me and shouted, "Malcolm!" Before she could say anything more, he said, "I know who it is. I can tell from the accent."

After that first meeting we visited one another's homes. She came over and made me a drizzle cake, which I'd never eaten before and I gave them some apple jam I'd made. And of course telling them about my agapanthus plants I gave them some for their garden. We kept in touch and in 2014 I invited them to Fairweathers Open Day, which was being held on the last weekend of July. They were both sorry they wouldn't be able to attend. I didn't hear from them again but got a call from Malcolm in November that she'd passed away. Of course that was why they were unable to come to the open day. I didn't know that she'd had cancer.

I'm so glad that I'd met her again and that we'd become friends.

Reds

After I'd brought Ashley to the UK and we were living in the flat I'd rented, I had a letter from my sister saying Redvers was arriving in the UK in the next week. She said my parents were at their wits' end not knowing what to do because he was out of control, and a family friend had said "buy him a ticket and send him to England". My father was a bit of a miser and it must have nearly killed him to withdraw the money for a plane ticket, so the situation must have been really bad for him to do so. But how he could have decided to send him over without a word to me beggars belief.

At first I didn't know what to do. For a start Reds and I never really got on. He was a reincarnation of Arthur, into drugs and drink, and I'd also have to remember that he was twice the size of me, so fisticuffs were off the agenda.

I had Alvin and Ashley with me and there was no way I could have him staying with us for the simple reason there wasn't any room for one more – and because of his lifestyle. I phoned Peter in London and told him the situation. He said not to worry, he'd go to Heathrow to meet him and take him back to his bedsit. They were roughly the same age, and although different in lifestyles, they both liked music and both played the guitar. Peter helped him find accommodation and he found employment as a train driver.

Redvers had had the best education – because of the type of friends he mixed with my parents decided to send him to a private school. It was called 'Little Flower' and was about 50 miles from Durban, but sadly it wasn't the making of him.

In London he sought out South Africans who enjoyed the same things he liked. He'd go down to the docks in London when there was a South African cargo ship in port and enjoy smoking dagga and bringing some back with him.

I was friends with an American girl at the time. Her dad worked for the United Nations. She was very posh and well educated. Redvers phoned and said he was celebrating his birthday and wanted me to come over. I wasn't keen on going, but Margaret was keen – I think because I'd told her about Redvers and I think she was curious and wanted to satisfy her curiosity. So off we went. You'd be forgiven if you thought you were back in South Africa and not London. I must admit I didn't feel comfortable at all. But Margaret was intrigued, what with the accents, because most of the guys were from the Cape and their accents were very much influenced by speaking Afrikaans. At one stage the guys were sitting in a circle (none of the girls were). There was a gadget that looked like the end of a bottle. This went round to each guy who took a swig and when it came to my brother's turn he took it and looked at me as much as to say "Don't you dare"! It was the first time I'd ever seen him take drugs. When it came to me I just shook my head.

Not long after that he left London and moved to Bristol. I invited my mum and sister over for a holiday. I was never keen on driving. By now I'd moved into my present home and I was with Annette. She was a very confident driver so she drove when we went to Heathrow. Redvers had decided he was going to Heathrow as well, travelling from Bristol by train. Just before the passengers came through we went to the Arrivals section. I could hear the sound of music coming from there and as we got closer I could see Redvers. He was sitting there, playing his guitar, his cooked chicken and cider beside him. Although everyone seemed amused, I wasn't. I tried to hide behind Annette. I might have felt a little different if he'd been sober. Annette just took it in her stride. That was one of the qualities I loved about her, nothing ever fazed her. Even on holiday in Durban at the snake park she was one of the first to let a python wrap itself around her.

It was great to see Mum and Pinky and soon we were back home. John Nesbit and his wife Patty, with whom I'd stayed when he worked in the Transkei, had come back to the UK with their two children. They were staying with us at first but then moved across Southampton Water to the village of Fawley where his mum still lived and they rented a house there. Redvers stayed with Ashley at his home.

One day Redvers turned up and somehow or other he and Pinky started arguing with each other. My mum said, "You two have come all the way from South Africa to fight in Kenny's home. You should be ashamed of yourselves." I was always called Kenny in South Africa but from the day I landed in the UK no one ever called me by that name, which was an abbreviation of Kenneth. But thankfully Pinky and Reds didn't come to blows.

Friends of my parents had emigrated to the UK and were living in Southend. My mum was keen to see them and since we'd also decided to visit Peter and his family in Ramsgate we decided to drive there. We now owned a two year old Ford and Annette loved driving it. We had lunch at friends of my mum in Southend and then went on to Ramsgate. Peter was over the moon at seeing her. He insisted she stay there while Annette and I found a guesthouse nearby. We really enjoyed our stay at Peter and Pam's home, and Mum took a photo of herself with their two daughters, Charlotte and Jemma. On the way back we used the minor roads, stopping off at one of the delightful pubs where we had a bit to eat and Mum (I always called her Amelia) enjoyed a beer. Of her time here on holiday I think the visit to Peter and Pam in Ramsgate was the most enjoyable.

It was in February 1990. I was working on the ferries in Felixstowe. I'd work two weeks on and two weeks off. On this occasion when I got home Annette said somone had called from Bristol but wouldn't give her any information but asked her to tell me to call him as soon as I arrived home.

Instinctively I knew it must have something to do with Redvers. I phoned this guy and he said Redvers had terminal cancer and hadn't long to live. We'd had bad weather and some trees had fallen across roads so we decided we'd go by train rather than drive. When we arrived at the hospital we expected to see him in bed in a ward, but he was sitting outside enjoying a cigarette. Honestly, he looked the picture of health. It was hard to take in what the doctor had said. He said they'd asked him if he'd like to have chemotherapy but he declined, saying he'd rather not. I said I'd visit him the following week and he asked me to bring him a pair of large pyjamas. Ashley and his wife Molly also visited him and it all seemed weird that this healthy-looking guy was at death's door.

The following week, the day before I was due to visit him, we received a call saying he'd passed away, before I could even give him his pyjamas. Back to Bristol Annette and I went to arrange the funeral. I don't know how I'd have coped without Annette. Redvers didn't have any possessions, just his guitar and motorbike, which he'd asked his friend to have.

A few months later I decided to visit my family and my mum asked me if I'd bring Red's ashes back to her. I enquired at South Africa House if there'd be a problem and they said it would be okay. On the flight over there was a lot of turbulence and when I saw my mum I joked that if something had happened it wouldn't just have been me, but Redvers as well. Sadly she died the following year.

Blind date

It was 1976, the year Southampton Football Club (The Saints) won the FA Cup, and being a Saints fan I made sure I was at Wembley. Friends of mine worked at the firm AC Delco. I asked Dorothy (my friend) if she knew of any unattached girls who worked there and if she could fix me up with a blind date. This she arranged.

I'd only just learned to drive a couple of years earlier. Just imagine me, a panel beater working with cars from the age of 16 (when not at sea), and not being able to drive. Unbelievable. I'd bought a three-wheeler from this ship's engineer who wanted to buy a 'Bond Bug', also a three-wheeler but more classy. If it wasn't for that reason I still probably would have never learned to drive and then I'd never have met Annette. Gosh.

It never entered my head that my blind date might not be too happy being picked up by a middle-aged guy driving a Robin Reliant. At least I took her to Southampton's poshest nightclub, 'The Silhouette'. We married in 1980. I took her to South Africa a number of times where we toured the Wild Coast and Swaziland. She really enjoyed these holidays. Then my mum and sister came here to the UK. My mum was pleased to see Ashley again. It has been quite a long journey for me. But all in all I think I achieved what it was I wanted for myself and my son. Now in the year 2017 my immediate family are no more (my generation that is). In South Africa there is just my Aunt Peggy who turned 101 this September. I shall phone her on Christmas Day.

Here in the UK it is Dennis and me. He still lives in Leicester and has family there and two grandchildren. We speak at least once a week on the phone, most of the time about our boyhood days. Sadly Peter died in 2012. He was happily married with two children and lived in Ramsgate. Unlike Dennis, who visited South Africa on a number of occasions, Peter never ever went back. But his brother and two sisters did come over here for a holiday so that made him happy.

I see my two great-grandchildren often, watch Saints Football Team play every home game (I'm a season ticket holder) and my hobby is still breeding agapanthus, lavatera and crocosmia flowers. The days of breeding chickens are over. Anyway, where I live the crowing of roosters at dawn would not be tolerated by the neighbours.

My mum with Peter's two daughters when she visited Peter in Ramsgate

True Saints Fan

The year was 1964. I was working as a panel beater for a firm which was just around the corner from where the stadium is now. I'd arrived in the UK a few years earlier from Durban in South Africa and had never been to a football match.

A young apprentice asked me if I'd like to go with him to a match at the Dell, and I said, "What? Stand for two hours watching a football match?" He said he'd get two seats in the stands and I said okay.

I enjoyed it so much that when the Saints played their next game at home I went on my own, getting there early so that I could stand by the low wall with no one in front of me.

I also attended the game at Brisbane Road when Terry Paine scored the goal that secured our promotion. I had a job keeping up with the young guys I went with, what with trying to find parking for the van we drove up in, getting there late and missing the goal. In fact we couldn't see much anyway because we were stood right at the back. What a night.

One night (I think Liverpool was the team we were playing) the stadium was full to the rafters and halfway through the second half I needed a pee. I looked behind me and all I could see was a sea of faces. I knew I'd never make it to the toilets, and even if I did I'd never get back, so I suffered in silence and at the end ran all the way home, luckily just six to eight minutes away. There is more to this story but not for print.

After that experience I decided to make something to stand on which fitted into a bag. From then on I got to the match ten minutes before kick-off, stood at the back on my box and was head and shoulders above everyone else. Problem solved.

I then became a season ticket holder, sitting under the main stand with my seat fifteen rows up along the centre line. I also attended both finals at Wembley.

Season ticket holders were told that when the new stadium was ready we'd be given like-for-like seats. While the stadium was being constructed I used to go there on average twice a week. I made friends with one of the guys there and at times he'd give me a hard hat and show me around. I looked at the Kingsland stand fifteen rows up along the centre line, and thought, like-for-like, wonderful.

When I did get my new seat it was way up in the stand near the Northam end. I wasn't happy with that and after a couple of games I went to the Stadium and complained. The guy I spoke to took me into the empty stadium and asked me where I'd like to sit. The seat I showed him was already taken but the end seat just three seats away was mine if I wanted it. It's turned out to be the best seat ever. I don't have to stand up for anyone. I just turn around. No problem.

My brother-in-law, who now lives in the USA, used to be a Saints fan. He bred a racehorse there, brought it over, and asked

Saints if he could race it in Saints colours. They agreed. He called it Southampton Joe. It won a few races and was also mentioned in one of the programmes. There was also a picture of the horse winning one of its races in one of the lounges.

I am now 87, a widower, and Saints and my hobby of breeding Agapanthus flowers are my main interests. I never miss a home match.

What would I most like to do? I'd like to visit Staplewood training ground when it's finished. I used to watch football there before Saints took it over. If I remember rightly the team was called Road Sea Southampton.

Am I a Saints fan? Most certainly. YES YES YES.

Days of wine and roses

It was the year 1964. Ashley and I were living in the ground floor flat. The upper flat was occupied by a middle-aged couple. The back garden was quite large and the agreement was that we'd each have the use of half of it. But the couple upstairs weren't interested in using their half.

Because I'd always been interested in my grandad's rose garden I started planting roses. I ended up with around 20, all different, and in bloom they looked quite spectacular. Ashley came home from school one day with a small plant that had been grown in the classroom from seed. I instantly recognised it as being a grape vine. I thought vines couldn't be grown in the UK because of the cold winters, but nevertheless I put it out in the garden. It lost all its leaves over the winter and I thought it had died, but as winter turned into spring it suddenly sprang back into life.

For the next four years it grew but never produced flowers or fruit. It was during the summer of 1968 just before I was due to exchange contracts for the home I was moving into, that Muriel told me the new tenants upstairs wanted their half of the garden straight away. I told her it was the middle of summer, the roses were in full flower, and it was the wrong time to be digging them up. She said that if I didn't do so, the next time I came the new tenants would probably have dug them up anyway.

I spoke to the young couple who were selling me their home and they said it was okay for me to dig a large trench in which to put my plants. Back I went to the flat, dug up all my roses, put them in the trench, half covered them with soil, and that is how they stayed until I moved in a month or so later. In the event those tenants never ever used the garden and there was no need to dig up my plants.

Fortunately I only lost about four plants. When I moved to my present home I started all over again with roses. My number one favourite, one called 'Papa Mielland', was a deep velvety red, almost black, and it had the best scent of any rose I've ever had.

One day, in one of the national papers, I saw an article on winemaking and growing grapes. And the book about it all was called 'Vine-growing in Britain Today' by Gillian Pearkes. I bought the book. It was very informative and also gave names and addresses of people who grew vines in the UK. I saw one had an address in Leicester and wondered how far it was from where Dennis lived. I got on a train to visit Dennis and when I asked him how far away this address was, he said quite near in fact. So off we went and found the address. I was expecting to see a vineyard, but they were all just semi-detached houses. I thought we might have got the wrong place, but knocked on the door. The owner opened it and said, "Come in, I'll be delighted to show you my vines."

The back garden had nothing but grape vines. It was late summer and there were bunches of black, green and pink looking grapes. He said he had 12 different varieties, outdoor and greenhouse, for eating and winemaking. I asked him if I could buy some cuttings when he pruned them and when he told me what it would cost –

"just a few shillings" – I said I'd like two of each. He said he'd post them to me just before the beginning of spring.

Come spring he posted them to me. Not two of each variety but four: 48 in all. What with moving house and lots of other things to do, I hadn't done much work in the garden, not having prepared it for grapes anyway. I put two of each variety separately and the rest were just mixed together.

Every single cutting grew. I was giving plants to guys on the ship (I was on the ferries from Weymouth to the Channel Isles), to the station masters at both stations and anyone else who showed the slightest interest in grape vine growing. I kept one of each variety, two in the greenhouse – they were the eating grapes – and the others outdoors. After three years I had my first grapes. I still had my rose bushes. Annette was now with me (she wasn't keen on roses because of the thorns); it was before the agapanthus-crocosmia-lavatera era.

I now had the winemaking bug: read books on how to make wine; bought all the necessary things – jars, fermenting gadgets etc. I'm afraid it's so long ago now that I've forgotten most of the names of the things I used. Suffice to say some of the wine was awful, some good, and some very good. One lot tasted like vintage champagne. And try as I could I was never able to make the same again.

I had them bottled and labelled, then I decided to make strawberry vodka. It had a fantastic taste but was very rich.

One evening Alvin came over. I asked him if he would like a bottle of wine to take home. He said he'd like that. So I said we'd have a drink first to see if he liked it. That was a red wine. I then asked if he'd like a white to take home. Yes, he said. I said we'd taste that one too to see if he liked it. Which of course he did. By now we were both feeling merry. Annette had gone to bed because she was doing a part-time job the next morning and in any case she wasn't into drinking alcohol. I then asked Alvin had he ever drank strawberry vodka. "Strawberry vodka? I've never heard of it; I'd love to try some."

He liked it so much he asked if he came over with some strawberries would I make him some. I agreed. His wife Trisha had dropped him off, so I phoned for a taxi to take him home, because I didn't dare disturb Annette, and because she wouldn't have been amused at the state I was in. I decided to sleep in the spare room. Before I knew it, she was standing in front of me with a cup of coffee and saying she was off to work and how disgusting I looked, still half drunk.

A little while later I was still in bed when the doorbell rang. I put on a dressing gown and went downstairs, looking and feeling awful. Opening the door, who should I see there? Alvin and his two young children, each with a bag of strawberries. Alvin looked a picture of health, whereas I felt as though I were at death's door. That was the last time I ever suffered a hangover.

Gradually, over the years, I started losing interest in winemaking and also the taste of alcohol. I've been teetotal for years now. Not even merry at Christmas.

I did make the strawberry and vodka drink for Alvin as I'd promised. How could I refuse?

Ashley, Tracy and Warren

My journey with Agapanthus, Crocosmia and Lavatera Flowering Plants

Besides watching my local football team and enjoying time spent with my two great-grandchildren, breeding agapanthus and lavatera plants gives me loads of pleasure. I can spend as much time as I like at Fairweathers Nursery, so thank you, Patrick, Sharon, Lisa and the staff with whom I have a fantastic relationship. I'm fortunate to enjoy something I love doing, which started as a youngster. Has the journey ended? Definitely not.

It all began on a holiday to Durban, South Africa, in the country's summer in December. Durban is my birthplace and I was visiting relatives.

ProVaR

HOME   ABOUT ProVaR   ProVaR PLANTS   NEWS   **TRADE INFO**   LINKS   CONTACT

Plant Breeder Profiles

KEN RIGNEY

As a youngster growing up in Durban, South Africa, I was always interested in gardening. I was greatly influenced by my Grandfather, whose passion was roses.

Settling in the UK revived my interest in gardening. On holidays to South Africa I would return with seeds of Agapanthus, Crocosmia and Zantedeschia and of any unusual plants that caught my eye. I would select the plants I wanted to breed from, isolate them from the others, and with a tiny brush and the help from some obliging bees, cross my fingers and hope. From this method along came an Agapanthus which caught my eye as it came into bud, first looking as blue, and then seemingly white. Once they fully opened I realised it was the first bicolour agapanthus I'd ever seen. An enigma? Hence the name Agapanthus Enigma. Another success is Agapanthus Snow Pixie.

I had a number of Lavateras growing in large pots and once again using my tried and tested method of pollination I was ecstatic when I saw Lavatera Red Rum for the first time, with it's deep reddish pink flowers and almost black stems. My family will insist that Red Rum was named after a famous racehorse, but my version is that when I was much younger and working in the merchant navy we were given a daily tot of rum, when diluted with a dash of blackcurrant, lemonade and ice, it was most enjoyable. The colour of that drink is exactly that of Lavatera Red Rum.

In a modest back garden tucked away in a suburban Southampton street something is stirring that has sparked interest from around the world.

The biggest names in horticulture from around the world have been left in awe by the floral specimens that have been grown in an ordinary suburban garden in Southampton by former merchant seaman Ken Rigney. Keith Hamilton, right, reports

Former merchant seaman 75-year-old Ken Rigney loves nothing better than pottering about amongst his plants, snipping leaves here and plucking flowers there, and now years of patience have paid off as the global horticultural industry beats a path to his door.

When it comes to Crocosmias, Lavateras and Agapanthus then Ken is your man. What he does not know about these plants really is not worth cultivating.

Now Ken and the plants he has bred are recognised by the top horticultural authorities in this country and the USA. His species are protected by law around the globe.

It was in the 1980s while Ken was back home in Durban, South Africa visiting relatives that, by pure chance, he noticed a small corm on the ground.

"I picked it up and put in my pocket and never thought any more about it until I discovered it again in my trousers back in Southampton," said Ken, who has lived in Southampton since 1956.

Always a keen gardener, Ken thought he would try and bring on the corm, so he planted it in his garden and waited for something to happen.

"Sure enough up it came and it was like nothing I had seen before," said Ken. Crocosmias grow everywhere in South Africa but this was different so I took a bit of time over it and the plant came on wonderfully.

"To me this is what makes gardening so fascinating, when you spot something that is different, not what you expect, and then try to repeat the process.

"Anyway, I took the plant along to a car boot sale and showed it to a man selling plants and he too said that he had seen nothing like it before so I began to realise that I might have something a bit special."

Now, after years of breeding trials

carried out not only in his back garden but also under the strict scrutiny of the Royal Horticultural Society experts as well as the horticulturalists at Fairweather's Garden Centre at Beaulieu, Ken has developed his very own Crocosmia which is called

Golden Ballerina.

Ken has been awarded official EU and UK Plant Breeders' Rights, similar to a patent, over his creation that is being introduced to the nation's gardeners this year ready for next year's season.

"I nearly gave up at one point but I decided to battle on and now it has been worth every minute. There has been a lot of interest as it is a striking plant. The bright orange petals reflex back, looking like a ballet dancer's tutu, and the flower has a long stamen," said Ken, who worked on board the former Union-Castle ships as well as Cunard's Queen Mary.

"I have no idea how many plants might be sold by the nursery but I suppose it could be about 15,000 a year, but I really have no idea."

The interest in Golden Ballerina has now spread to the other side of the world in New Zealand as well as Japan in the Far East.

Not satisfied with this blooming success, Ken now has another three different Crocosmias under development that he hopes will come on the market in the not too distant future.

Crocosmia come mainly from mainly from South Africa, where they are often pollinated by sunbirds in the wild, but they are also found in Malawi, Swaziland and Tanzania.

On the west coast of the USA they have become an invaluable plant for attracting hummingbirds by providing them with a rich source of nectar.

It was a similar story when it came to Ken's Lavatera, which he has named Red Rum and that is now being sold in the UK as well as France and the US.

"It's a hardy shrub with dark stems and deep pink flowers which is again different from other Lavateras," said Ken, who receives a helping hand with his plants from his wife Annette.

Lavateras are an old cottage garden favourite thought to have been introduced into England as long ago as the 15th century from the Mediterranean where it grows in fields and on rocky slopes.

Ken has also had further success in developing two distinctive Agapanthus that he has called Snow Pixie and Enigma.

Agapanthus, which originate in South Africa, are popular with gardeners everywhere and the plant is also known as the Lily of the Nile, the Flower of Love and the African Lily.

"Snow Pixie is a small pure white plant, now on sale in Britain and the subject of American Plant Breeders' Rights, while I am still working on Enigma, which is bi-colour with blue and white, and I think it will be another two years before it goes on sale commercially," said Ken.

"Gardening is just a wonderful hobby and I suppose I caught the bug when I was a child back in Durban, where I would watch my grandfather look after his plants. I am really chuffed after all these years that plants I have bred are going to be enjoyed by gardeners around the world."

BEAUTIFUL BLOOMS: Ken pictured left with his Enigma flowers. Above left – the Golden Ballerina which started Ken's collection.

Echo pictures by Gordon Agg-Jones
Order no: rad376b3 (left), rad9eaa4 (above)

As a youngster growing up I was always interested in gardening (as well as pets and chickens), being influenced by my grandfather who was a keen rose grower. Flowers which also flourished in his garden were agapanthus.

Agapanthus Enigma bred by Ken Rigney

On this particular occasion I was walking along the embankment where the agapanthus were in full flower, some having already made seed. I'd never seen agapanthus in the UK and wondered whether they'd survive in our northern climate, especially through the winter. I picked up a few seeds and brought them home to see if I could get them to grow. A handful of them germinated, which I potted on, nurtured them through the winter and then after three years saw my first flowers. Some blue, some white, tall and medium. Because I wasn't sure whether they'd survive out in the garden in our winter, I decided to try out an experiment with my first blue agapanthus, which I called Blue Colossus.

I bought a huge umbrella from a car boot sale, cut off the material and covered it with plastic and put it over the agapanthus, staking it on all sides to prevent the wind from lifting it, and then taking it off in the summer – and it thrived and flowered. After a couple of years my wife said I should remove it (the umbrella) as passers-by would think there was someone weird living there. I still have Blue Colossus but not the original plant.

Two years ago I offered a lady who lives further up the road a plant and she said she remembered seeing the umbrella when she took her children to school. It made my day that someone had actually remembered seeing it all those years ago.

By cross-pollinating the different ones I had which I thought were exceptional I bred probably the world's first true bi-colour, which, because it happened by chance, my late wife named it Enigma.

Enigma was registered at the RHS Wisley in 1998 and grew in the gardens. In hindsight I should never have done that as seeds could be taken quite easily from the flowers, and up until then there were no bi-colour agapanthus that I knew of.

The other two at Wisley were Blue Colossus and Snow Pixie (Snow Pixie went on to obtain the American Patent, which protects the plant for 20 years).

Enigma has been sold commercially by Fairweathers Nursery in Hampshire since 2006 and is still selling now in 2017. There are now quite a few bi-colours on the market, but I'm proud of the fact that mine was the first.

In 1984, while on holiday in South Africa, we visited friends who lived in the Transkei. One day my host said he knew there was a lychee fruit orchard in the vicinity. Off we went but were unable to find it; however, when my host enquired of a local of its whereabouts, I waited by the car for him to return. This was in an isolated place, just trees and bushes, but no plants or flowers of any kind. I noticed a small black shiny pea-like seed on the ground, and picked it up, wondering what it was, and put it in my pocket. In the event we never did find the orchard, but when I returned home and was opening my pockets prior to using the washing machine, I saw the little black seed I'd picked up. I put it in my greenhouse and it grew and flourished. I put it out into the garden and over the years it flowered. I didn't pay much attention to it but knew it was part of the Crocosmia family.

In the late 1980s I used to take my two grandchildren to the local car boot sale, selling fuchsia and strawberry plants. To make my pitch interesting to customers I found that by cutting holes in containers and creating detachable inserts, I could plant a number of different varieties of fuchsia in one container. This led to me perfecting the idea of using containers suited to the purpose. Eventually I applied for and was granted a British patent for my invention, but try as

I might I was unable to get anyone to take it on, although one of the largest plant container manufacturers said I could use their products to convert them into my design, which I declined as I was doing it manually (which was hard work).

Dear Readers

The summer is over it seems, having stayed just too briefly in June and July.

I was to sample some of the very worst of the weather in August, when I took a trip to and from Zeebrugge, and spent a rather soggy day in the lovely city of Bruges.

The rain was lashing down, as the passengers embarked on both the outward and return journey. Many were soaked to the skin, and quite down in the mouth.

Added to that, both crossings were full, and I must congratulate the crew on their unfailing cheerfulness and courtesy as they dealt with dozens of wet, hungry and tired passengers, and maintained a cheerful welcome for everyone.

Its an attitude that was remarked on by the passengers I spoke to, and one which says a lot about our staff.

Do keep in touch, I really enjoy hearing from you.

Best wishes

Vivienne

Copydate for next issue 4th December.

All correspondence, articles or telephone calls to:

Vivienne Maunder
Marriott Howard Publicity
630 Woodbridge Road
Ipswich IP4 4PG
Tel: 0473 715556
or KNOLLINE 0473 270755
(24 hr ansaphone)

Ken has a patently delicious idea

Ken Rigney and his grandchildren Tracy and **W**arren love strawberries. So much so that Ken has grown his own for some years now.

Becoming increasingly frustrated by the upright strawberry growing containers when the plants fell out, he decided to design his own.

Several years on, and several hundred pounds lighter in the pocket, Ken, a motorman in the engine room of the Pride of Flanders, has patented his idea.

Where conventional strawberry growing containers have cut outs for the plants to grow from, Ken has added clip-on cups, which support the plants.

Up to now he's been buying containers at trade price, and hand crafted the product. And indeed he's enjoyed considerable success selling through mail order and on our ships.

But to really get the project off the ground he needs to make big investment in tools and moulding equipment, and he's currently facing an obstacle in that a major manufacturer is claiming the idea for itself.

For the time being though, Ken's idea is not only satisfying his culinary requirements - but also has given him a strong sense of personal achievement "Not everyone gets to take out a patent in their lifetime," he said.

While working in the Merchant Navy for P&O Ferries their magazine did an article on my invention. It was also featured in Amateur Gardening magazine. On googling my name recently I came across my invention (which by now is no longer protected).

Crocosmia Golden Ballerina

One morning at the car boot sale a customer came up to me and we started chatting about plants in general. He then invited me to visit his home to show me some of his plants. I said I'd take him up on the offer. A few weeks later I contacted him to arrange a visit. This was at the beginning of August 1994, and the plants that had been growing in my garden over the years were just beginning to flower. I shall never know what made me cut a flowering stem to show this guy, but as soon as he saw it, he asked where I'd got it. I told him from my garden. He was most insistent on where I'd originally got it from, and I told him how I'd found the seed in 1984 and that it had been in my garden ever since.

Flower and Strawberry Container

He then said it was a crocosmia and that he was very knowledgeable on crocosmias and that he'd never seen one like mine before. He told me to contact a nursery in Hampshire which might be able to identify it for me.

In the event I went to this nursery taking another cut flower and they identified it as Crocosmia Aurea. This variety grows wild in South Africa but aren't suited to our winters and even if they do survive the winters will flower so late in the year that frost won't allow the flowers to develop. The first question he asked me was whether it was hardy and I told him it was because it had been in my garden since 1984. He then said after they'd flowered I should contact him again and that I should dig up as many bulbs as I could.

At car boot sale

Midnight Madness.

Monday, September 8, 2014 **DAILY ECHO**

fb.com/dailyecho **News** Follow us on Twitter @dailyecho

SOUTHAMPTON: Vauxhall Astra crashes through wall into garden

Two hurt as car skids 70ft along on its side

DRAMA: The emergency services at the scene in St George's Avenue. Inset, the morning after.
Pictures: Thanks to Barbara Gammon.

On arriving home, my Amateur Gardening magazine had just been delivered, dated 13th August 1994 (I still have it). There was an article about a well-known nursery near Chichester that trialled unusual plants for amateur breeders. I contacted the nursery, taking another flower stem and driving the 50 miles to the nursery. The first thing they wanted to know was whether it was hardy. That is when I realised though there were other crocosmias that looked identical to mine, mine was unique in that it was hardy. I decided to apply for plant breeder rights and in my application told them how I had acquired the plant and that because the seed was found where there were no other plants, it was either there from a bird dropping or being blown by the wind and therefore a new variety. It took more than three years of examination by the PBR people (they obtained different varieties similar to mine to trial) and eventually I was granted PBR in 1999.

Because it had long delicate petals and a long stamen, Annette said it looked like a ballerina's tutu. She suggested calling it Golden Ballerina. Today Golden Ballerina is sold in the USA, Europe and Japan. Over here Fairweathers Nursery sell it.

In my garden grew lavateras, and one day I noticed a lavatera seedling which looked to have much darker stems, was more compact, and the flowers were a deeper magenta than most others. I showed this plant to Fairweathers Nursery in the New Forest. They assessed the plant for a few years and liked it. It was also sent to the USA where it was granted a United States patent, and an EU Plant Breeders' Rights Certificate in the UK.

Annette said she'd like it to be called Red Rum, which I agreed to call it. But not as she thought it was being named after a famous

racehorse. My version is that during my merchant
were given a tot of rum which I thought tasted av
mine with blackcurrant and lemonade, making i
tasting drink. The colour of that drink was identical
of Lavatera Red Rum. That is my side of it anyway.

[Back t(

On the Provar website the story of Enigma and R
found together with a picture of Yours Truly.

I a

Plant Breeders' Rights

Certificate No: **6933**

PLANT VARIETY RIGHTS OFFICE

Plant Breeders' Certificate

Kenneth Rigney
137B King Georges Avenue
Regents Park
Southampton

A variety of **Crocosmia aurea** known as **GOLDEN BALLERINA**

The Controller of Plant Variety Rights is satisfied that the conditions laid down in section 4 of the Plant Varieties Act 1997 have been fulfilled as respect "the breeder" and "the variety" and hereby Grants to the above named person **PLANT BREEDERS' RIGHTS** in respect of the variety in accordance with the Plant Varieties Act 1997 for a period of **twenty five** years from the **first day of April 1999.**

Signed

on this twelfth day of April 1999 for and on behalf of the Controller of Plant Variety Rights

n still trying to produce new varieties of agapanthus, crocosmias and lavateras, and Fairweathers Nursery continue to assess some of my seedlings, which they think might be of commercial interest. Among my other successes I have obtained PBR for Agapanthus 'Snow Pixie' and Lavatera 'Magenta Magic'.

It was during the time Enigma was growing at Wisley that I received a letter from Henry Rasmussen who lived in Pietermaritzburg, which just happens to be an hour's drive from Durban.

In the letter he introduced himself as an amateur breeder of agapanthus and said he had contacted Wisley to ask them if they knew of any agapanthus breeders in the UK. As I'd registered my plants there they gave him my address.

He said he'd bred a miniature agapanthus only 8" tall – did I think it was unique and could there be any future for it? He then sent me pictures of the plant and I was amazed. I showed the pictures to Patrick at Fairweathers and they were very interested in it.

The result of all that is that I was soon on my way to South Africa to see Henry as well as my family. Patrick had given me all the relevant paperwork to take with me. Plants would have to be cleaned and passed by South African customs. There was so much I was beginning to learn about plants, not just breeding them at home.

Henry was 91 years old when I met him. He and his wife Kay lived in a beautiful house with acres of garden in the affluent suburb of Hilton. In the three years I got to know him we became big friends, shared an affinity with flowers and my one regret is that I hadn't met him a few years earlier. He died in 2005. Henry was born in Denmark, came to the UK as a young man and worked in nurseries. He eventually left to live in South Africa. In the short time I got to know him I used to stay there when plants were dug up, divided, cleaned and then inspected by the Government Plant people to make sure they were OK to bring to the UK. Because he was Danish, he said he'd like the plant to be called Thumbelina.

Fairweathers grew the plant, put it in their catalogue, describing it as bred by Henry Rasmussen of South Africa. I took him the catalogue when I went back to see him and he was most pleased to see a picture of his plant and his name as the breeder of one of the smallest agapanthus ever bred. Hopefully Thumbelina will sell for years and years to come.

Midnight Madness

Sunday September 7th, 2014

A night and day to remember because of my home nearly being demolished by a drunken driver and also because it was the day my Aunt Peggy (last remaining relative of my generation living in South Africa) turned 98.

After Annette died I slept in the back bedroom of the house because it was away from the noise of the cars passing by and I could sleep undisturbed. I was woken suddenly by a huge noise. Just a loud bang then silence. I looked at my bedside clock and it was just after midnight. After a minute or two (I don't actually know how long) I got out of bed and, going into the front room, saw lights flashing. I ran to the top of the stairs and saw this blurred image in front of the frosted glass, and my first impression was that a helicopter had landed in my front garden. I rushed back into the bedroom, put some clothes on, ran down the stairs, opened the door and saw this car on its side with the door left open. (This is what made me think of the helicopter.)

By then people from the neighbouring streets were there. So was the ambulance, fire brigade and police. Someone must have contacted them immediately for them to have arrived so quickly.

It was like a scene from a movie. I saw my friendly neighbour across the road and went and stood next to him. It was as though it was someone else's house I was looking at. I can't describe it, but I had no feelings whatsoever.

Apparently there were three young people in the car, two boys and a girl. All under the influence of liquor. The 18 year old owner was in the back of the car. His friend, also under the influence and unlicensed, was driving. Goodness knows what speed he must have been doing, because he hit a car 70 yards away on the other side of the road, it turned on its side and hit my wrought iron gates and brick wall full on, demolishing everything. The back of my late wife's Micra was smashed, the dividing wall of my neighbour completely gone and also their bay window and brickwork smashed.

They arrested the driver. The guy in the back was screaming for help. The firemen had to cut the car to get him out. Fortunately, for them, they weren't seriously injured. Through all this I just stood there, not showing any emotion. I just can't explain it. Maybe I was in shock. After they'd taken away the car and the crowd had gone there were just these two policemen. I had my prize agapanthus in large pots in a small section of the garden and these guys said they'd help me take them to the back of the house as they were quite valuable to me.

Then by 3am or 4am (I'm not sure) I was all alone. My son lived on the other side of Southampton and my two grandchildren lived a little distance away as well, and I saw no point in calling them at four in the morning. Most of the day my neighbour and I cleared some of the rubble and broken bricks away. By late afternoon I suddenly remembered my aunt's birthday, and telephoned her. Of course I didn't mention the previous night's happening at all.

The insurers said my wife's Micra was a complete write-off, but having spent years working as a panel-beater I disagreed and said I'd have it repaired myself. It had only done 20,000 miles and, although a 1998 model, was in showroom condition. What they were offering to pay was a pittance. I'd never be able to get another decent car. My godson's brother, who is also a panel-beater, repaired it, and after being examined by the insurers' people it passed its MOT. The insurance company paid for the repairs. I still have the car. It's in pristine condition and has only done 26,000 miles. I use it for best, and use my 1986 Ford Escort for plants and all other dirty jobs. I've had it since 1988 so it's becoming a classic. People have made me offers for it but for as long as I can I'll keep it or until I'm told it's not roadworthy any more.

The one policeman, James Fibbens, who is my grandson's age, has become a great friend of mine and ever since that night of madness he pops over to see how I am getting along. He's very impressed with my agapanthus breeding programme as his 102 year old Nan is still tending her own garden, so I've given him a couple of plants for her. My neighbours are now quite used to seeing a police car outside my home. And drivers tend to slow down when they see it.

Two weeks before this incident, Patrick Fairweather, of Fairweathers Nursey, said one of my agapanthus he was trialling looked promising and that the public on the Open Day were quite impressed with it. It is a large deep electric blue that really stands out. Patrick said I should start thinking of a name for it. The next time I met him I said that if he decided to go ahead with it, I'd like it to be called 'Midnight Madness'.

Agapanthus Midnight Madness was launched at Fairweathers' Open Day on July 29th, 2017. It will be in the 2019 catalogue and

Before

After

I will be applying for EU Plant Breeders Rights. If all goes to plan and they are as good as we expect them to look then hopefully they will be sold countrywide and become successful. If that happens at least some good would have come out of it all.

I did phone my aunt on her 100th birthday and told her all about it and she thought the name of the flower very appropriate. Ever since that night, when I wake up at six in the morning to walk for a paper, I look at the Micra and the Escort to make sure they're OK. I don't know why but I've never replaced the wrought iron gates.

The Apartheid Laws and how they affected families' lives

Big Daddy had a sister whom I never met but whose name was 'Sweetie'. When she had a disagreement with her husband she'd come to my grandmother 'Tuku Mama' (who was black) for tea and sympathy. But after she divorced her husband, she remarried and became the mayoress of a small town in the Transkei, and from then on never set foot in my grandad's home again.

Years later, Pat, my mum's youngest brother (who was quite headstrong), went to see some friends who lived in this town, and they decided to go for a drink. There was a partition which separated the whites from mixing with the non-whites.

Of course Pat went straight into the white side. He was just being served when this white guy came over and said he wasn't allowed there. Pat was having none of it and a scuffle started. His friends had to get him out before the situation worsened, and got out of hand. It was quite a while later that his friends told him that the guy who tried to have him thrown out was 'Sweetie' the mayoress' son. Pat's first cousin. Imagine if Pat had known that then and said, "My dad and your mum are brother and sister" – and he would have, had he known. And how would his white cousin have felt?

There were lots of situations of people I knew, where some things that happened in their lives had a sad ending.

Alfred Jannaman came to Durban with an illness from his home in

94

Bizana. He was treated as a white with his family visiting him all being white, but when they realised he was dying, his mother, who was mixed race, was brought to see him as his nanny.

There were other situations which were quite hilarious were it not for the serious consequences that followed. One such instance was a friend of mine, whose family all passed as white. He was on his way home one night a little the worse for wear. He got off the train and along the pathway met a black woman. They were in a compromising situation when they were pounced on by the police and arrested. Rather than tell the authorities that he was of mixed race and therefore not breaking the Apartheid Law, he went to prison for four months and that was because he wanted to protect his family, all of whose lives would have changed completely had he admitted his mixed blood parentage. Years later he met and fell in love with a mixed race girl, and asked to be reclassified as Coloured, which they did, and he married her.

My sister-in-law's mother was a widow. Her mother's new partner was white and they had a daughter. Once the police found out about this, they wasted no time in doing their duty. They didn't even bother to visit them in the daytime (because then they could have said her partner was just visiting). They waited till nightfall to catch them in bed and hauled them before the courts. Cynthia's older sister took her half-sister to live with her while her mother and partner served their prison sentence. Once out they were back together again. Again they were sent to prison. The authorities then decided to leave them alone if he classified himself as non-white, which he did. And they lived happily ever after.

That's true love for you.

The worst thing about the Apartheid regime was what they did to my brother-in-law's family. Cocky Winkworth – he who gave a party to the crew for looking after Mrs Winkworth and their daughter when they sailed back to Durban after holidaying in the UK.

This didn't affect my decision to leave South Africa because unlike the other happenings this occurred after I'd left the country, and it was when I was in the Merchant Navy and visiting Durban that I was told all about it. Everyone called him Cocky. He was Cocky to business associates as well as staff who worked for him. He owned race horses and lived in one of the exclusive areas on the Bluff. The famous South African jockey Charlie Barends rode one of his winners.

Cocky and his brother who lived nearby married two sisters. They were of St Helena heritage and looked Mediterranean in appearance. It was at the party at his home that I first met the crew of the Cape Town Castle.

Cocky died and six months later his brother died. It was just a few months later that both sisters were told to sell up and leave as they weren't allowed to live there, under the Group Areas Act.

While Cocky and his brother were alive there wasn't a problem, but once they'd died they were told to vacate their homes.

The camp that once housed the British Personnel during the war was now a sort of council estate run by the council for the poorer mixed race people. The sisters had to live in one of these houses. Even my parents said how could the authorities be so cruel.

My brother-in-law bought a house for them on the other side of Durban and I did visit them. They were such good people and so well brought up, and didn't show any hatred at all. But I bet inwardly they were very sad at how their lives had changed.

Years later, after the end of apartheid, Derek and my sister and I drove past his boyhood home. We stopped the car and looked up at the house and wondered if the people who lived there knew its story. The Black Government was telling people who felt they'd been affected by the previous government's apartheid laws that they could see if they could claim compensation. But Derek and Pinky (now in middle age) felt it was too long ago. I did hear their children were thinking of looking into it, but I don't think anything came of it.

Yes, Dr Malan and Dr Verwoerd have a lot to answer for. Lots and lots of families, not just around me, but in the rest of South Africa as well, families that were torn apart, where suicides occurred, people imprisoned because of their love for someone. I am one of the lucky ones who was able to leave before it wrecked my and my son's life. As it surely would have done had we stayed. The simple fact is that we'd still be in the same city as the other half of the family who were white, and who knows how it might have ended.

In her mid-80s now, my first wife still keeps her secret life to herself.

Will her family ever know the truth? Not from my side I don't think. Their lives are now English and British I'm happy to say.

My colourblind childhood has now ended with me finding colour in breeding flowers in adulthood.

Ken with Agapanthus (Midnight Madness)